You're a Big Hit, Charlie Brown!

You're a Good Man, Charlie Brown!

Music and Lyrics by CLARK GESNER

Based on the comic strip "PEANUTS"
by CHARLES M. SCHULZ

A FAWCETT CREST BOOK
Fawcett Publications, Inc., Greenwich, Conn.

CAUTION

Professionals and amateurs are hereby warned that *YOU'RE A GOOD MAN, CHARLIE BROWN*, and the characters and other material from the comic strip and cartoon entitled PEANUTS being fully protected under the Copyright Laws of the United States of America, the British Commonwealth including the Dominion of Canada and all other countries of the Berne and Universal Copyright Conventions, is subject to royalty. All rights including professional, amateur, motion picture, recitation, lecturing, readings, radio and television broadcasting, adapting and the rights of translation into foreign languages are strictly reserved.

Application for stage presentation is to be made to Tams-Witmark Music Library, Inc., 757 Third Avenue, New York, New York 10017.

THIS BOOK CONTAINS THE COMPLETE TEXT OF THE ORIGINAL HARDCOVER EDITION.

A Fawcett Crest Book reprinted by arrangement with Random House, Inc.

Library of Congress Catalog Card Number: 68-14529

Photographs by courtesy of Peanuts Company

Printed in the United States of America

For

Sparky

FOREWORD

When *Charlie Brown* went into rehearsal on February 10, 1967, there was no script. There were ten songs, a few long scenes, two producers, one small theatre, six medium-sized actors, one each of director, assistant director, writer, musical supervisor, lighting designer and scenic designer, ten years' worth of Charles Schulz's drawings, and one purpose. The purpose was to put "Peanuts" onstage.

When the show opened on March 7, 1967, there still was no script but "Peanuts" was onstage, so nobody much cared. This published edition is, in effect, a description, written after the fact, of what finally wound up on that stage after everyone had done the best he could in his particular department to accomplish that single purpose. If the play has managed to succeed, it stands as one more tribute to Charles Schulz's immensely human view of the world and his special ability to say it for all of us.

The official credits for *You're a Good Man, Charlie Brown* list John Gordon as the author of the "book." This name is what might be called a collective pseudonym standing partly for myself, who set the words down, and partly for the people mentioned above, who created the event.

C.G.

Above: The cast as drawn by Charles M. Schulz.

Right: The cast as it appears on the stage of the musical entertainment.

YOU'RE A GOOD MAN, CHARLIE BROWN *was first presented on March 7, 1967, by Arthur Whitelaw and Gene Persson at Theatre 80 St. Marks, in New York City.*

CAST OF CHARACTERS

LINUS

CHARLIE BROWN

PATTY

SCHROEDER

SNOOPY

LUCY

Book by John Gordon
Directed by Joseph Hardy
Assistant to the Director Patricia Birch
Musical Supervision, Arrangements and Additional Material by Joseph Raposo
Sets and Costumes by Alan Kimmel
Lighting by Jules Fisher
Piano Ronald Clairmont
Percussion Lou Nazarro

MUSICAL NUMBERS

ACT ONE

You're a Good Man, Charlie Brown	Entire Company
Schroeder	Lucy, Schroeder
Snoopy	Snoopy, Charlie Brown
My Blanket and Me	Linus
The Kite	Charlie Brown
Dr. Lucy (The Doctor Is In)	Lucy, Charlie Brown
Book Report	Charlie Brown, Lucy, Linus, Schroeder

ACT TWO

The Red Baron	Snoopy
T.E.A.M. (The Baseball Game)	Entire Company
Glee Club Rehearsal	Entire Company
Little-Known Facts	Lucy, Linus, Charlie Brown
Suppertime	Snoopy
Happiness	Entire Company

ACT ONE

Time: An average day in the life of Charlie Brown.

Just as the audience is beginning to be aware that there is the faint sound of a funny little waltz coming from somewhere, the house lights begin to dim. The darkness increases, the waltz moves and grows, and then a single light picks out a small face at center stage. It is CHARLIE BROWN. *Suddenly the music stops, and a voice pipes up from the darkness behind him.*

LINUS

I really don't think you have anything to worry about, Charlie Brown. After all, science has shown that a person's character isn't really established until he's at least five years old.

CHARLIE BROWN

But I *am* five. I'm more than five.

LINUS

Oh. Well, that's the way it goes.

(The waltz continues. It glides forward, rises, then stops again)

PATTY

(From another section of the darkness)

The only thing wrong with Charlie Brown is his lack of confidence. *(She thinks a moment)* His inferiority and his lack of confidence. *(She thinks again)* His clumsiness, his inferiority and his lack of confidence. *(She pauses again)* His stupidity, his clumsiness, his inferiority and his . . .

(The music mercifully begins again, cutting off her speech. It trickles along briefly, then stops)

SCHROEDER

Did you know that Charlie Brown has never pitched a winning baseball game, never been able to keep a kite in the air, never won a game of checkers and never successfully punted a football? Sometimes I marvel at his consistency.

(The music begins again. It rises to a brief pause)

LINUS

I think Charlie Brown has nice hands.

(The music continues to another stopping place)

SNOOPY

It is truly a dog's life. I feel so neglected. Charlie Brown never brings me coffee in the morning.

(The music is heard for another moment)

LUCY

Now, Linus, I want you to take a good look at Charlie Brown's face. Would you please hold still a minute, Charlie Brown, I want Linus to study your face. Now this is what you call a Failure Face, Linus. Notice how it has failure written all over it. Study it carefully, Linus, you rarely get to see such a good example. Notice the deep lines, the dull, vacant look in the eyes. Yes, I would say this is one of the finest examples of a Failure Face that you're liable to see for a long while.

(The music fades as CHARLIE BROWN *stirs himself to speak)*

CHARLIE BROWN

Some days I wake up early to watch the sunrise, and I think how beautiful it is, and how my whole life lies before me, and I get a very positive feeling about things. Like this morning, for instance. The sky's so clear and the sun's so bright. How can anything go wrong on a day like this?

(His question is answered by an ominous and energetic imitation of drum taps from SCHROEDER *and* LINUS. *The stage is suddenly filled with light and we at last can see its contents: several oversized, brightly painted objects in simple geometric shapes, and six undersized, simply dressed people of straightforward, uncomplicated character. As the music swings into a march, the people begin parading around and about the rather nonplused fellow at center stage. They sing "You're a Good Man, Charlie Brown")*

ALL
(*Except* CHARLIE BROWN)

You're a good man, Charlie Brown,
You're the kind of reminder we need.
You have humility, nobility and a sense of honor.
That are very rare indeed.
You're a good man, Charlie Brown,
And we know you will go very far.
Yes, it's hard to believe,
Almost frightening to conceive,
What a good man you are.
You are kind to all the animals
And ev'ry little bird.
With a heart of gold you believe what you're told.

LUCY

Ev'ry single solitary word.

ALL

You bravely face adversity,
You're cheerful through the day,
You're thoughtful, brave and courteous.

LUCY

And you also have some faults, but for the
Moment let's just say . . .

ALL

That you're a good man, Charlie Brown,

(They break into a boisterous march)

You're a good man, Charlie Brown,
You're a prince, and a prince could be king.
With a heart such as yours
You could open any doors,
You could go out and do anything.
You could be king, Charlie Brown,
You could be king!

LUCY

If only you weren't so wishy-washy.

(The music and the marchers disappear as quickly as they arrived, and as the sound of a jangling school bell cuts through the fading voices, CHARLIE BROWN *is left alone at center stage, seated, clutching a paper bag)*

CHARLIE BROWN

I think lunchtime is about the worst time of the day for me. Always having to sit here alone. Of course, sometimes mornings aren't so pleasant, either—waking up and wondering if anyone would really miss me if I never got out of bed. Then there's the night, too—lying there and thinking about all the stupid things I've done during the day. And all those hours in between—when I do all those stupid things. Well, lunchtime is *among* the worst times of the day for me.

Well, I guess I'd better see what I've got. *(He opens the bag, unwraps a sandwich, and looks inside)* Peanut butter. *(He bites and chews)* Some psychiatrists say that people who eat peanut butter sandwiches are lonely. I guess they're right. And if you're really lonely, the peanut butter sticks to the roof of your mouth. *(He munches quietly, idly fingering the bench)* Boy, the PTA sure did a good job of painting these benches. *(He looks off to one side)* There's that cute little redheaded girl eating her lunch over there. I wonder what she'd do if I went over and asked her if I could sit and have lunch with her. She'd probably laugh right in my face. It's hard on a face when it gets laughed in. There's an empty place next to her on the bench. There's no reason why I couldn't just go over and sit there. I could do that right now. All I have to do is stand up. *(He stands)* I'm standing up. *(He sits)* I'm sitting down. I'm a coward. I'm so much of a coward she wouldn't even think of looking at me. She hardly ever *does* look at me. In fact, I can't remember her ever looking at me. Why shouldn't she look at me? Is there any reason in the world why she shouldn't look at me? Is she so great and am I so small that she couldn't spare one little moment just to . . . *(He freezes)* She's looking at me. *(In terror he looks one way, then another)* She's *looking* at me.

(His head looks all around, frantically trying to find something else to notice. His teeth clench. Tension builds. Then, with one motion, he pops the paper bag over his head. LUCY *and* PATTY *enter)*

LUCY

No, Patty, you're thinking of that other dress, the one I wore to Lucinda's party. The one I'm talking about was this very light blue one and had a design embroidered around the waist.

PATTY

I don't remember that dress.

LUCY

(Takes a pencil and draws matter-of-factly on the bottom of the paper bag)

Something like this. The skirt went out like this and it had these puffy sleeves and a sash like this.

PATTY

Oh yes, I remember.

LUCY

Yes, well *that* was the dress I was wearing last week when I met Frieda and she told me she'd seen one just like it over at . . .

(The girls have exited. CHARLIE BROWN *sits immobile as their voices fade)*

CHARLIE BROWN

(The paper bag still pulled over his head)

Lunchtime *is* among the worst times of the day for me. If that little redheaded girl is looking at me with this stupid bag on my head she must think I'm the biggest fool alive. But if she isn't looking at me, then maybe I could take it off quickly and she'd never notice it. On the other hand, I can't tell if she's looking until I take it off. Then again, if I *never* take it off, I'll never have to know if she was looking or not. On the other hand, it's very hard to breathe in here. *(There is a moment of tense silence. Then his hand rises slowly, jerks the bag from his head and folds it quickly as he glances furtively in the direction of the little girl. He smiles)* She's not looking at me. *(He looks concerned)* I wonder why she never looks at me. *(The school bell jangles once again)* Oh well, another lunch hour over with. Only two thousand, eight hundred and sixty-three to go.

(As he makes his way offstage, the opening bars of Beethoven's "Moonlight Sonata" are heard and a change in lighting reveals SCHROEDER *and* LUCY *on another part of the stage.* SCHROEDER *is seated at one of the shapes which somewhat resembles a piano. He is engrossed in his playing.* LUCY *is leaning contentedly against the "piano," listening. In counterpoint to the continuing sonata, she sings "Schroeder")*

LUCY

(Singing)

D'ya know something, Schroeder?
I think the way you play the piano is nice.
D'ya know something else?
It's always been my dream that I'd marry
A man who plays the piano.
At parties he'd play something nice
Like "April Showers."
I'm sure you could play something nice
Like "April Showers."
Or even "Frere Jacques."
Beethoven's nice, too.

Just imagine.
What would you think if someday you and I should get
married?
Wouldn't you like that if someday we two should get
married?

(SCHROEDER *hasn't heard a word she's said. His playing finally reaches a pause in the music)*

LUCY

My Aunt Marion was right. Never try to discuss marriage with a musician.

(With the final chords of the piece, the light slowly fades. Then, upstage, suddenly there is PATTY*)*

PATTY

(Standing at attention with her hand over her heart)

I pledge allegiance to the flag of the United States of America, and to the Republic for which it stands. One nation, under God, indivisible, with liberty and justice for all. *(She sits, then quickly stands again)* Amen.

*(*CHARLIE BROWN *and* LINUS *enter at another corner of the stage.* CHARLIE BROWN *is looking at a large, stiff, brightly colored square of board which is, of course, a newspaper)*

CHARLIE BROWN

I think most of us take newspapers too much for granted. We don't really appreciate the miracle that is the modern daily newspaper. Of course, it's difficult to put into words just why one likes a newspaper.

LINUS

I like a newspaper because you don't have to dial it.

(CHARLIE BROWN exits. LINUS, holding his blanket, sits quietly at center stage. LUCY casually wanders by, then makes a quick grab for his blanket and takes off with it)

LUCY

I got it! I got it!

LINUS

(Going after her like a shot)

You give me back my blanket.

LUCY

No! I've got it and I'm going to keep it. *(They stop running)* This is just the start you need to help you break this disgusting habit.

LINUS

Apparently you haven't read the latest scientific

reports. A blanket is as important to a child as a hobby is to an adult. Many a man spends his time restoring antique automobiles, or building model trains, or collecting old telephones, or even studying about the Civil War. This is called playing with the past.

LUCY

Really?

LINUS

Certainly. And this is good, for it helps these men to cope with their everyday problems. Now, I feel that it is going to be absolutely necessary for me to get my blanket back, so I'm just going to have to give it a good YANK! *(He quickly pulls the blanket away from her)* It's surprising what you can accomplish with a little smooth talking and some fast action.

(From behind the largest object on the stage, something that could easily be mistaken for a doghouse, SNOOPY *appears. He is a human being, like any other dog, and he happens to be wearing a white turtleneck sweater, black pants and sneakers. He*

yawns, stretches and walks downstage, where PATTY *sees him)*

PATTY

Oh, Snoopy, you're such a sweet doggy. I'd love to give you a great big kiss. (SNOOPY *offers a pucker)* But of course I can't.

(She quickly crosses away)

SNOOPY

The curse of a fuzzy face.

(He sinks into a resigned heap on the floor. The light reveals PATTY *and* LINUS *seated together)*

LINUS

Happiness is a fleeting thing, Patty, but I think that a man can really come closer to it by directing the forces of his life towards a single goal that he believes in. And I think that a man's personal search for happiness is not really a selfish thing, either, because by achieving happiness himself, he can help others to find it. Does that make sense to you?

PATTY

We had spaghetti at our house three times this week.

(A burst of virtuoso piano playing mercifully draws our attention to another part of the stage where SCHROEDER *is once again practicing and* LUCY *is once again talking)*

LUCY

What would you think, Schroeder, if someday you and I got married and we were so poor you had to sell the piano to buy me saucepans?

(The music comes to a sour halt)

SCHROEDER

Saucepans?

LUCY

Well, sure. You don't expect me to set up housekeeping without a good set of saucepans, do you?

SCHROEDER

Saucepans?

LUCY

Well, girls have to think about those things. Boys are lucky. Boys never have to think about things like saucepans.

SCHROEDER

(Rises, crosses slowly away)

I can't stand it. I just can't stand it.

(He collapses with his head in his hands)

SNOOPY

(Moving forward, jaw jutting, brow furrowed. He himself up to his full height)

Here is the fierce jungle ape pounding his mighty chest while the other animals cower in the distance. Now he throws back his head and emits a terrifying roar . . . arf! *(He collapses in complete chagrin)* How humiliating.

(He drags himself up onto his doghouse. PATTY enters, walking slowly, staring at the limp jumprope she holds in her hand)

SCHROEDER

What's the matter, Patty?

PATTY

Well, I don't know. I was jumping rope. Everything was all right, and suddenly, it all seemed so futile.

(She exits. SNOOPY *rises on his doghouse, and with musical support assumes three highly dramatic and impressive poses. Then he stops)*

SNOOPY

I would have made a terrific trophy.

(He lies down. LUCY *enters, fit to be tied, and shouting angrily offstage)*

LUCY

It's not fair! You promised me a birthday party and now you say I can't have one. It's not fair! IT IS NOT FAIR!

LINUS

You're not using the right strategy.

LUCY

What?

LINUS

The more you fuss, the worse off you'll be. Why not admit it was all your own fault. Why not go up to Mom and say to her, "I'm sorry, dear Mother. I admit I've been bad and you were right to cancel my party. From now on I shall try to be good." That's much better than ranting and raving. All that does is prove her point.

LUCY

(Thinks a moment, then tries it on for size)
"I'm sorry, dear Mother. I admit I've been bad and you were right to cancel my party. From now on I shall try to be good." *(She smiles at the effort, starts offstage, stops, and then returns to* LINUS*)* I'D RATHER DIE!

(They exit. SCHROEDER *is left on the stage, which he paces contentedly)*

SCHROEDER

Beethoven loved the country. He quite often liked to take long strolls into the countryside. He loved the peace and quiet of the country. They were an inspiration to him.

LUCY

(Offstage)

Gimme that ball, you blockhead!

SCHROEDER

Beethoven had it nice.

(The lights dim as he exits. Then SNOOPY, *asleep on the doghouse, can be seen squirming and whimpering with delight at the sound of the following dialogue which, at the moment, is brightening his dreams)*

CHARLIE BROWN

(Offstage)

Hey, Snoopy, we're home from school. Hi there, fella. Gosh, it's good to see you.

LUCY

(Offstage)

Oh, Snoopy, you're so adorable. Mm-mm!

CHARLIE BROWN

Okay, Snoopy, get back on your doghouse. I'll be out later with your supper.

LUCY

I think Snoopy's such a wonderful dog.

CHARLIE BROWN

I do too. He's just about the best there is.

(The music begins, the lights grow. SNOOPY *stirs, stretches, and happily considers his situation. He sings "Snoopy")*

SNOOPY

(Singing)

They like me,
I think they're swell.
Isn't it remarkable
How things work out so well?
Pleasant day, pretty sky,
Life goes on, here I lie.
Not bad, not bad at all.
Cozy home, board and bed,
Sturdy roof beneath my head.
Not bad, not bad at all.

Faithful friends always near me,
Bring me bones, scratch my ear.
Little birds come to cheer me,

Every day
Sitting here
On my stomach
With their sharp little claws
Which are usually cold
And occasionally painful,
And sometimes there are so many
That I can hardly stand it . . .

Rats!
I feel ev'ry now and then that I gotta bite someone.
I know ev'ry now and then what I wanna be,
A fierce jungle animal crouched on the limb of a tree.
I'd stay very very still till I see a victim come.
I'd wait, knowing very well ev'ry second counts,
And then, like the fierce jungle creature I am,
I would pounce.
I'd pounce.
I'd pounce.
I'd . . .

You know, I never quite realized it was so far down to the ground from here. Hm.

Let me see, where was I?

Oh, that's right. The pretty sky.
Not bad, not bad at all.

I wonder if it will snow tonight.

(He grumbles a moment to himself, then falls asleep. The lights change. CHARLIE BROWN *enters, holding his paper bag)*

CHARLIE BROWN

I think I'll walk right up to that little redheaded girl and introduce myself. I think I'll introduce myself and then I think I'll ask her to come over here and sit by me. I think I'll ask her to sit by me and then I think I'll tell her how much I've always admired her . . . I think I'll flap my arms and fly to the moon.

(He exits. SNOOPY *rouses himself and starts to ease over the rear edge of his house, pondering as he goes)*

SNOOPY

Yesterday I was a dog. Today I'm a dog. Tomorrow I'll probably still be a dog. There's just so little hope of advancement.

(He is gone. The lights ruminate a moment,

then reveal a shadowy figure with a blanket. After ably dispatching an invisible insect with a quick snap of the blanket, LINUS *settles down with his woolly companion in front of the TV set. The music of "My Blanket and Me" begins. The first pause of the song is punctuated by his contented sigh, the second by his murmuring "delightful" as he fondles the blanket. Eventually he is moved to sing)*

LINUS

(Singing)

It's a cozy sanctuary
But it's far from necessary
'Cause I'm just as self-reliant as before.
As a simple demonstration
Of my independent station
I will go and leave my blanket on the floor.
Yes, I'll walk away and leave it
Though I know you won't believe it
I'll just walk away and leave it on the floor.

(He saunters away, humming. The hum grows tenser, however, and soon, unable to bear the separation any longer, he makes

a desperate grab for the blanket)

Don't ever let me do that again.

(The music resumes. LINUS *dances with his "friend")*

Got you back again.

(The music continues and grows. Finally . . .)

It's foolish, I know it,
I'll try to outgrow it,
But meanwhile
There's my blanket and me.

(He sighs. As the song ends, LINUS *is once again settled in front of the TV.* LUCY *enters and watches with him for a moment)*

LUCY

Okay, switch channels.

LINUS

Are you kidding? What makes you think you can come right in here and take over!

LUCY

(Holding out her hand)

These five fingers individually are nothing. But when I curl them together into a single unit they become a fighting force terrible to behold.

LINUS

Which channel do you want? *(He looks at his hand)* Why can't you guys get organized like that.

LUCY

Linus, do you know what I intend? I intend to be a queen. When I grow up I'm going to be the biggest queen there ever was, and I'll live in this big palace with a big front lawn, and have lots of beautiful dresses to wear. And when I go out in my coach, all the people . . .

LINUS

Lucy.

LUCY

. . . all the people will wave and I will shout at them, and . . .

LINUS

Lucy, I believe "queen" is an inherited title. *(*LUCY *is silent)* Yes, I'm quite sure. A person can only become a queen by being born into a royal family of the correct lineage so that she can assume the throne after the death of the reigning monarch. I can't think of any possible way that you could ever become a queen. *(*LUCY *is still silent)* I'm sorry, Lucy, but it's true.

LUCY

(Silence, and then)

. . . and in the summertime I will go to my summer palace and I'll wear my crown in swimming and everything, and all the people will cheer and I will shout at them . . . *(Her vision pops)* What do you mean I can't be a queen.

LINUS

It's true.

LUCY

There must be a loophole. This kind of thing always has a loophole. Nobody should be kept from being a queen if she wants to be one. IT'S UN-DEMOCRATIC!

LINUS

Good grief.

LUCY

It's usually just a matter of knowing the right people. I'll bet a few pieces of well-placed correspondence and I get to be a queen in no time.

LINUS

I think I'll watch television.

(He returns to the set)

LUCY

I know what I'll do. If I can't be a queen, then I'll be very rich. I'll work and work until I'm very very rich, and then I will buy myself a queendom.

LINUS

Good grief.

LUCY

Yes, I will buy myself a queendom and then I'll

kick out the old queen and take over the whole operation myself. I will be head queen. And when I go out in my coach, all the people will wave, and I will . . . I will . . .

(She has glanced at the TV set and become engrossed. Pretty soon LINUS *turns and looks at her)*

LINUS

What happened to your queendom?

LUCY

Huh?

LINUS

What happened to your queendom?

LUCY

Oh, that. I've given it up. I've decided to devote my life to cultivating my natural beauty.

(As LINUS *looks at her in disbelief, the scene disappears into blessed darkness. Then quick, urgent music is heard and* CHARLIE BROWN *lurches in from the wings, strug-*

gling with an invisible kite on the end of an invisible string. He sings "The Kite")

CHARLIE BROWN

(Singing)

Little more speed, little more rope,
Little more wind, little more hope,
Gotta get this stupid kite to fly.
Gotta make sure it doesn't snag,
Doesn't droop, doesn't drag,
Gotta watch out for ev'ry little—whoops!

Little less speed, little more tack,
Little less rise, little more slack,
Gotta keep my wits about me now.
Gotta make sure it doesn't get the best of me
Till I get it in the air somehow.

Millions of little kids do it ev'ry day,
They make a kite and "poof," it's in the sky.
Leave it to me to have the one fool kite
Who likes to see a little kid cry.

Little less talk, little more skill,
Little less luck, little more will,

Gotta face this fellow eye to eye.
Now that I've seen you chasing moles,
Climbing trees, digging holes,
Wrapping your string on everything passing by,
Why not fly?

Wait a minute.
What's it doing?
It isn't on the ground,
It isn't in a tree,
It's in the air.
Look at that, it's caught the breeze now,
It's past the trees now, with room to spare.

Oh, what a beautiful sight.
And I'm not such a clumsy guy,
If I really try
I can really fly a . . .

(A terrible rending of paper and wood is heard. CHARLIE BROWN *watches as his imaginary string goes limp. He slumps, heaves a small sigh of resignation, and heads doggedly for the exit as the music chases him out.* PATTY *walks pertly onstage with a large pencil and a flat, brightly colored*

board which is, of course, a letter she is writing)

PATTY

Dear Ann Flanders. Last year I sent fifty-two valentines and received seventy-five. This year I sent fifty-eight valentines and only received sixty-one. Am I right in blaming this on the zip code?

(She exits. CHARLIE BROWN *enters, carrying an envelope. He practices presenting it)*

CHARLIE BROWN

This is for you, Lucy, happy Valentine's Day. That doesn't sound right. Here, Lucy, this is for you, happy Valentine's Day. You can do it if you just don't get nervous. This is for you, Lucy, happy Valentine's Day. *(*LUCY *enters.* CHARLIE BROWN *quietly reassures himself)* Okay, just take it easy, you can do it. *(Aloud)* This is for you, Lucy. *(He gives her the card)* Merry Christmas.

(In an instant he realizes what he's done and collapses with a moan. PATTY *enters counting valentines. She happens to drop one as she passes* CHARLIE BROWN*)*

PATTY

Hi, Charlie Brown.

CHARLIE BROWN

Hi, Patty. Oh, wait a minute, you dropped something. Say, what is all this?

PATTY

Valentines. They're for all the boys in our class at school that I like.

CHARLIE BROWN

Well, we wouldn't want to lose this one, would we? With the initials C. B. on it.

PATTY

No, I guess not. Craig Bowerman would be very disappointed.

CHARLIE BROWN

I can't stand it.

*(*PATTY, LUCY *and* SCHROEDER *congregate upstage, exchanging cards)*

CHARLIE BROWN

Look at them, laughing and enjoying themselves with their valentines. I sent a valentine to everyone I know this Valentine's Day, and did I get any in return? No, not one. I did not get a single valentine. Everybody gets valentines but me. Nobody likes me. I get about as many valentines as a dog. (SNOOPY *walks by counting a large batch of valentines)* My stomach hurts. (CHARLIE BROWN *heads for the wings. The others also exit. The lights and music then cheerily accompany* LUCY *as she goes about some sort of business at one corner of the stage. She finally flips a sign in place reading "The Doctor Is In," and we see that she has set up her booth for psychiatric help.* CHARLIE BROWN *enters, wretched)* Oh, Lucy, I'm so depressed. Everything is going wrong. I don't know what to do.

LUCY

I'm sorry to hear that, Charlie Brown. Maybe there's something I can do to help. I think what you need most of all is to come right out and admit all the things that are wrong with you.

CHARLIE BROWN

Do you really think that will help, Lucy?

LUCY

Certainly.

CHARLIE BROWN

All right, I'll try.

(They sing "The Doctor Is In")

CHARLIE BROWN

(Singing)

I'm not very handsome, or clever, or lucid,
I've always been stupid at spelling and numbers.
I've never been much playing football, or baseball,
Or stickball, or checkers, or marbles, or ping-pong.
I'm usually awful at parties and dances,
I stand like a stick, or I cough,
Or I laugh,
Or I don't bring a present,
Or I spill the ice cream,
Or I get so depressed that I
Stand and I scream,
Oh, how could there possibly be

One small person as thoroughly, totally, utterly
Blah as me.

LUCY

Well, that's okay for a starter.

CHARLIE BROWN

A starter?

LUCY

Well, sure. You don't think that mentioning these few superficial failings is going to do any good, do you? Why, Charlie Brown, you really have to delve.

(She sings)

You're stupid, self-centered and moody.

CHARLIE BROWN

I'm moody.

LUCY

You're terribly dull to be with.

CHARLIE BROWN

Yes, I am.
And nobody likes me.
Not Frieda, or Shermy, or Linus, or Schroeder . . .

LUCY

Or Lucy.

CHARLIE BROWN

Or Lucy.

LUCY

Or Snoopy.

CHARLIE BROWN

Or Sn—

Now wait a minute. Snoopy likes me.

LUCY

He only pretends to like you because you feed him. That doesn't count.

CHARLIE BROWN

Or Snoopy.

Oh, why was I born just to be
One small person as thoroughly, totally, utterly . . .

LUCY

Wait.
You're not very much of a person.

CHARLIE BROWN

That's certain.

LUCY

And yet there is reason for hope.

CHARLIE BROWN

There is hope?

LUCY

For although you are no good at
Music, like Schroeder,
Or happy, like Snoopy,
Or lovely, like me,
You have the distinction to be
No one else but the singular, remarkable, unique
Charlie Brown.

CHARLIE BROWN

I'm me!

LUCY

Yes, it's amazingly true.
For whatever it's worth, Charlie Brown,
You're you.

CHARLIE BROWN

Gosh, Lucy, I'm beginning to feel better already. You're a true friend, Lucy, a true friend.

LUCY

That'll be five cents, please.

(The lights dim. LUCY *exits.* SNOOPY *is seen seated at one side.* CHARLIE BROWN *greets him weakly before exiting, and one by one each of the other characters crosses the stage, patting* SNOOPY'S *head, or calling their greeting as they go by)*

CHARLIE BROWN

Hi, Snoopy. How's the fella?

PATTY

Hi, Snoopy. Cute doggy.

SCHROEDER

What d'ya say, tiger!

LUCY

Hi, fuzzy face.

LINUS

Hi, Snoopy.

SNOOPY

(Watches them go, then drags himself offstage, muttering)

Nobody ever calls me sugarlips.

*(A dour musical undercurrent begins and four gloomy-looking people—*LUCY, SCHROEDER, LINUS, *and* CHARLIE BROWN*—enter with pencils and "notebooks," taking their places at four different parts of the stage)*

ALL

Homework. Yeough!

(They sing "The Book Report")

LUCY

A book report on "Peter Rabbit."

LINUS

A book report on "Peter Rabbit."

SCHROEDER

A book report on "Peter Rabbit."

CHARLIE BROWN

A book report on "Peter Rabbit."

LUCY

(Thinks briefly, then . . .)

"Peter Rabbit" is this stupid book
About this stupid rabbit who steals
Vegetables from other people's gardens.

(She counts the words, one through seventeen)

Eighty-three to go.

SCHROEDER

The name of the book about which
This book report is about is
"Peter Rabbit," which is about this
Rabbit.
I found it very—

(He crosses out)

I liked the part where—

(He crosses out)

It was a—

(Slash!)

It reminded me of "Robin Hood."
And the part where Little John jumped from the rock
To the Sheriff of Nottingham's back.
And then Robin and everyone swung from the trees
In a sudden surprise attack.
And they captured the Sheriff and all of his goods,

And they carried him back to their camp in the woods,
And the Sheriff was guest at their dinner and all,
But he wriggled away and he sounded the call,
And his men rushed in and the arrows flew—
Peter Rabbit did sort of that kind of thing too.

LUCY

The other people's name was MacGregor.

(She counts the words from eighteen to twenty-three)

Hmm.

LINUS

In examining a work such as *Peter Rabbit*, it is important that the superficial characteristics of its deceptively simple plot should not be allowed to blind the reader to the more substantial fabric of its deeper motivations. In this report I plan to discuss the sociological implications of family pressures so great as to drive an otherwise moral rabbit to perform acts of thievery which he consciously knew were against the law. I also hope to explore the personality of Mr. MacGregor in his conflicting roles as farmer and humanitarian. (CHARLIE BROWN *begins to sing*) Peter Rabbit is established from the start as a benevolent hero and it is only with the increase of social pressure that the seams in his moral fabric . . .

CHARLIE BROWN

(LINUS' *speech fades as he begins to sing*)

If I start writing now
When I'm not really rested
It could upset my thinking
Which is not good at all.
I'll get a fresh start tomorrow
And it's not due till Wednesday,
So I'll have all of Tuesday
Unless something should happen.
Why does this always happen—
I should be outside playing,
Getting fresh air and sunshine,
I work best under pressure
And there'll be lots of pressure
If I wait till tomorrow,
I should start writing now.
But if I start writing now

When I'm not really rested,
It could upset my thinking
Which is not good at all.

LUCY

The name of the rabbit was Peter.
Twenty-four, twenty-five, twenty-six, twenty-seven,
Twenty-eight, twenty-nine, thirty.

SCHROEDER

Down came the staff on his head—smash!
And Robin fell like a sack full of lead—crash!
The Sheriff laughed and he left him for dead—ha!
But he was wrong.

LUCY

Thirty-four, thirty-five, thirty-six, thirty-seven,
Thirty-eight, thirty-nine, forty.

SCHROEDER

Just then an arrow flew in—whing!
It was the sign for the fight to begin—zing!
And then it looked like the Sheriff would win—ah!
But not for long.
Away they ran.

Just like rabbits,
Who run a lot,
As you can tell
From the story
Of "Peter Rabbit,"
Which this report
Is about.

CHARLIE BROWN

How do they expect us to write a book report . . .

LUCY

There were vegetables in the garden . . .

CHARLIE BROWN

. . . of any quality
In just two days.

LUCY

Such as carrots and spinach and onions and . . .

(CHARLIE BROWN *and* LUCY *sing simultaneously)*

CHARLIE BROWN

How can they
Conspire to make life so miserable

And so effectively
In so many ways.

LUCY

Lettuce and turnips and
Parsley and okra and cabbage and string beans
    and parsnips,
Tomatoes, potatoes, asparagus,
Cauliflower, rhubarb and chives.

LINUS

Not to mention the extreme pressure exerted on him by his deeply rooted rivalry with Flopsy, Mopsy and Cottontail.

*(*LUCY, CHARLIE BROWN *and* SCHROEDER *sing simultaneously)*

LUCY

"Peter Rabbit" is this
Stupid book
About a stupid
Rabbit who steals
Vegetables from other people's gardens.
Gardens, gardens.

Seventy-five, seventy-six,
Seventy-seven, seventy-eight,
Seventy-nine, eighty,
Eighty-one, eighty-two.

CHARLIE BROWN

If I start writing now
When I'm not really rested
It could upset my thinking
Which is not good at all.
No good at all.

Oh—

First thing after
Dinner I'll start.

SCHROEDER

The name of the book about which
This book report is about is
"Peter Rabbit, Peter Rabbit."
All for one,
Every man does his part.

Oh—

LUCY

And they were very, very, very, very,
Very, very happy to be home.

SCHROEDER

The end.

LUCY

. . . ninety-four, ninety-five.

(Singing)

The very, very, very end.

LINUS

A-men.

CHARLIE BROWN

(Beginning to write)

A book report on "*Peter Rabbit*"

BROWN, *who leaves his "desk" and wanders dejectedly downstage. He happens to look up, and in doing so, sees a single, large green leaf hanging just at the edge of the proscenium. He hesitates, then sees the audience and speaks to them)*

CHARLIE BROWN

You know, I don't know if you'll understand this or not, but sometimes, even when I'm feeling very low, I'll see some little thing that will somehow renew my faith. Just something like that leaf, for instance—clinging to its tree in spite of wind and storm. You know, that makes me think that courage and tenacity are about the greatest values that a man can have. Suddenly my old confidence is back and I know things aren't half as bad as I make them out to be. Suddenly I know that with the strength of his convictions a man can move mountains, and I can proceed with full confidence in the basic goodness of my fellow man. I know that now. I know it.

(With unfamiliar strength in his step, CHARLIE BROWN *turns and makes his way offstage, a glimmer of new hope in his eyes. Then, without even a respectful pause, the leaf promptly drops from its tree and wiggles its way to the ground)*

Curtain

ACT TWO

A throbbing rhythm from the percussion, a hint of "Over There" in the melody, a dimming of the house lights, and Act Two is under way. As the curtain opens we see a familiar figure silhouetted on the top of his doghouse, seated bolt upright, his arms outstretched before him, a scarf around his neck and the goggles of his leather helmet pulled down firmly over his eyes. The music and lights help SNOOPY *throughout in telling his story of bravery and heroism.*

SNOOPY

Here's the World War One flying ace high over France in his Sopwith Camel, searching for the infamous Red Baron. I must bring him down. Suddenly anti-aircraft fire, archie we call it, begins to burst beneath my plane. The Red Baron has spotted me. Nyahh, nyahh, nyahh! You can't hit me. (*Parenthetically*) Actually, tough flying aces never say "nyahh, nyahh." I was just, uh . . . (*Back to business*) Drat this fog. It's bad enough to have to fight the Red Baron without having to fly in weather like this. All right, Red Baron! Come on out. You can't hide from me forever. Ah! The sun has broken through. I can see the woods of Montsec below. But, what's this? It's a Fokker triplane. Ha, I've got you. You can't escape from me this time, Red Baron! Augh! He's diving down out of the sun. He's tricked me again. I've got to run. Come on, Sopwith Camel, let's go. Go, Camel, go! I can't shake him. He's riddling my plane with bullets. Curse you, Red Baron! Curse you and your kind! Curse the evil that causes this unhappiness. (*The tempo changes.* SNOOPY *relaxes, removing his goggles and scarf*) Here's the World War One flying ace back at the aerodrome in France. He is exhausted and yet he does not sleep, for one thought continues to throb in his brain: Someday, someday I'll get you, Red Baron!

(*He reclines in noble leisure as the music crashes to its final chords.* PATTY *enters, skipping rope. She circles the doghouse with exuberant energy)*

PATTY

All right, everybody out for rabbit chasing.

SNOOPY

Oh good grief.

PATTY

Let's go, Snoopy, up and at 'em. It's a magnificent day for chasing rabbits. The air is clear, the sun is shining, the fields and woodlands lie open and inviting.

SNOOPY

If it's such a magnificent day, why spoil it for the rabbits?

PATTY

Come on, Snoopy. Where's that old thrill of the chase? Where's your spirit of adventure? What kind of a dog are you, anyway?

SNOOPY

I am a sleeping dog. You take it from there.

PATTY

You should be ashamed of yourself, wasting a perfect day like this. The scent is fresh. The trail is clear. Let's get out there and track us down a big ol' rabbit.

SNOOPY

Well, I get the feeling she's determined. Okay, if that's what she wants, she might as well get her money's worth.

PATTY

Atta boy, Snoopy. I predict we'll see lots of game today (SNOOPY *takes a deep breath, scrambles from his doghouse and, with* PATTY *following behind, gives a short, furious and highly convincing display of "dog tracking down rabbit." He ends up panting in front of* PATTY) Well, I guess we're not going to find anything today, Snoopy. But at least you tried. Even though you've failed, it always makes you feel better when you know you've done your best.

(She exits)

SNOOPY

I'd hate to disillusion her, but I don't even know what a rabbit smells like.

(SNOOPY *retires to his house.* CHARLIE BROWN *enters, wearing a baseball cap and glove. He assumes his place on the pitcher's mound and begins his speech, in spite of the unnerving fact that no one is there to speak to)*

CHARLIE BROWN

All right, gang. I want this game to be our biggest and best game of the season, and I want everyone out there playing with everything he's . . .

(LUCY *comes onstage and approaches him)*

LUCY

Charlie Brown, I thought up some new strategy for you. Why don't you tell the other team that we're going to meet them at a certain place, only it isn't the real place, and then when they don't show up, we'll win by forfeit. Isn't that good strategy? (CHARLIE BROWN *is silent.* LUCY *starts to leave.*)

I don't understand these managers who don't want to use good strategy.

CHARLIE BROWN

The thing we have to remember is spirit and teamwork. If we all really grit our teeth and bear down I'm sure we can finish off this season with . . .

(SCHROEDER *comes onstage and approaches* CHARLIE BROWN. *The whole gang is now onstage, each wearing a baseball cap and glove)*

SCHROEDER

Charlie Brown, is Lucy going to pitch again? Because if she is, I quit. Do you know what she does? She's always calling me out for conferences on the mound. I go out there, see? I go out there for a secret conference on the mound and do you know what she does? She kisses me on the nose.

CHARLIE BROWN

If we really grit our teeth and bear down I'm sure we could finish this season . . .

LINUS

Perhaps you shouldn't be a playing manager, Charlie Brown. Perhaps you should be a bench manager.

PATTY

That's a good idea. You'd be a great bench manager, Charlie Brown. You could say "Bench, do this" or "Bench, do that." You could even be in charge of where we put the bench. When we get to the playing field, you could say, "Let's put the bench here" or "Let's put the bench there."

CHARLIE BROWN

I can't stand it.

LUCY

What's the sense of our playing when we know we're going to lose? If there was even a million-to-one chance we might win, it would make some sense.

CHARLIE BROWN

Well, there may not be a million-to-one chance,

but I'm sure there's at least a billion-to-one chance. Now come on, gimme a "T."

ALL

"T!"

CHARLIE BROWN

Gimme an "E."

ALL

"E!"

CHARLIE BROWN

Gimme an "A."

ALL

"A!"

CHARLIE BROWN

Gimme an "M."

ALL

"M!"

CHARLIE BROWN

Whaddaya got?

ALL

TEAM!

(They burst into "The Baseball Game")

ALL

(Singing)

There is no team like the best team,
Which is our team right here.
We will show you we're the best team
In the very Little League this year.
And in no time we'll be big time,
With the big league baseball stars,
For all we have to do is win just one more game
And the championship is ours.

(CHARLIE BROWN *is now on the opposite side of the stage from the rest of the team, who have frozen into a tableau of baseball pandemonium. He writes)*

CHARLIE BROWN

Dear Pen Pal,

(Singing)

You'll never guess what happened today
At the baseball game,
It's hard to believe what happened today
At the baseball game.
I was the manager,
Schroeder was catcher,
And all of the team was the same
As always but
Somehow or other disaster struck
At the baseball game.

ALL
(*Except* CHARLIE BROWN)

There is no team like the best team,
Which is our team right here.
We will show you we're the best team
In the very Little League this year.
And in no time we'll be big time,
With the big league baseball stars,

For all we have to do is win just one more game
And the championship is ours.

CHARLIE BROWN

Three balls, two strikes, the bases were loaded
With two men out.
I pitched my curve, but somehow he hit it
A good strong clout.
"Lucy," I hollered, "It's coming right to you."
She caught it as easy as pie—then dropped it;
I don't think it's good for a team's morale
To see their manager cry.
Snoopy helped out by biting a runner
And catching the ball in his teeth.
Linus caught flies from a third-story window
By holding his blanket beneath.
Yes, we had fortitude,
No one could argue with that.
And one run would win us the game as I came up to bat.

LUCY

(Speaking, as the others repeat their "fight" song)

All right, Charlie Brown, we're all behind you—sort of. Now get a hit, Charlie Brown. This guy can't pitch. He pitches like my grandmother. We know you can do it if you just grit your teeth and bear down. Please, Charlie Brown, please . . .

ALL

For all we have to do is win just one more game.

LUCY

And the championship is ours!

CHARLIE BROWN

Two men were on with two outs, and me with
One strike to go,
Then I saw her, this cute little redheaded
Girl I know.
Firmly I vowed I would win it for her
And I shouldered the bat and I swung . . .
Dear Pen Pal, I'm told where you live is
Really quite far.
Would you please send directions on
How I can get where you are?

Your friend,
Charlie Brown.

(The stage slowly darkens as the players

drag themselves off. Then SCHROEDER *and* LUCY *reenter upstage, minus their baseball equipment)*

SCHROEDER

I'm sorry to have to say it right to your face, Lucy, but it's true. You're a very crabby person. I know your crabbiness has probably become so natural to you now that you're not even aware when you're being crabby, but it's true just the same. You're a very crabby person and you're crabby to just about everyone you meet. (LUCY *remains silent —just barely*) Now I hope you don't mind my saying this, Lucy, and I hope you'll take it in the spirit that it's meant. I think we should all be open to any opportunity to learn more about ourselves. I think Socrates was very right when he said that one of the first rules for anyone in life is "Know thyself." (LUCY *has begun whistling quietly to herself*) Well, I guess I've said about enough. I hope I haven't offended you or anything.

(He makes an awkward exit)

LUCY

(Sits in silence, then shouts offstage at SCHROEDER*)*

Well, what's Socrates got to do with it anyway, huh? Who was *he* anyway? Did he ever get to be king, huh! Answer me that, did he ever get to be king! *(Suddenly to herself, a real question)* Did he ever get to be king? *(She shouts offstage, now a question)* Who *was* Socrates, anyway? (*She gives up the rampage and plunks herself down*) "Know thyself," hmph.

(She thinks a moment, then makes a silent resolution to herself, exits and quickly returns with a clipboard and pencil. CHARLIE BROWN *and* SNOOPY *have entered, still with baseball equipment)*

CHARLIE BROWN

Hey, Snoopy, you want to help me get my arm back in shape? Watch out for this one, it's a new fastball.

LUCY

Excuse me a moment, Charlie Brown, but I was wondering if you'd mind answering a few questions.

CHARLIE BROWN

Not at all, Lucy. What kind of questions are they?

LUCY

Well, I'm conducting a survey to enable me to know myself better, and first of all I'd like to ask: on a scale of zero to one hundred, using a standard of fifty as average, seventy-five as above average and ninety as exceptional, where would you rate me with regards to crabbiness?

CHARLIE BROWN

(Stands in silence for a moment, hesitating) Well, Lucy, I . . .

LUCY

Your ballots need not be signed and all answers will be held in strictest confidence.

CHARLIE BROWN

Well still, Lucy, that's a very hard question to answer.

LUCY

You may have a few moments to think it over if you want, or we can come back to that question later.

CHARLIE BROWN

I think I'd like to come back to it, if you don't mind.

LUCY

Certainly. This next question deals with certain character traits you may have observed. Regarding personality, would you say that mine is *A* forceful, *B* pleasing, or *C* objectionable? Would that be *A*, *B*, or *C*? What would your answer be to that, Charlie Brown, forceful, pleasing or objectionable, which one would you say, hmm? Charlie Brown, hmm?

CHARLIE BROWN

Well, I guess I'd have to say forceful, Lucy, but . . .

LUCY

"Forceful." Well, we'll make a check mark at the

letter *A* then. Now, would you rate my ability to get along with other people as poor, fair, good or excellent?

CHARLIE BROWN

I think that depends a lot on what you mean by "get along with other people."

LUCY

You know, make friends, sparkle in a crowd, that sort of thing.

CHARLIE BROWN

Do you have a place for abstention?

LUCY

Certainly, I'll just put a check mark at "None of the above." The next question deals with physical appearance. In referring to my beauty, would you say that I was "stunning," "mysterious," or "intoxicating"?

CHARLIE BROWN

(Squirming)

Well, gee, I don't know, Lucy. You look just fine to me.

LUCY

(Making a check on the page)

"Stunning." All right, Charlie Brown, I think we should get back to that first question. On a scale of zero to one hundred, using a standard of fifty as average, seventy-five as . . .

CHARLIE BROWN

(Loud interruption)

I . . . (*quieter*) . . . remember the question, Lucy.

LUCY

Well?

CHARLIE BROWN

(Tentatively)

Fifty-one?

LUCY

(Noting it down)

Fifty-one is your crabbiness rating for me. Very well then, that about does it. Thank you very much for helping with this survey, Charlie Brown. Your cooperation has been greatly appreciated.

(She shakes hands with CHARLIE BROWN*)*

CHARLIE BROWN

(Flustered)

It was a pleasure, Lucy, any time. Come on, Snoopy.

LUCY

Oh, just a minute, there is one more question. Would you answer "Yes" or "No" to the question: "Is Lucy Van Pelt the sort of person that you would like to have as president of your club or civic organization?"

CHARLIE BROWN

Oh, yes, by all means, Lucy.

LUCY

(Making note)

Yes. Well, thank you very much. That about does it, I think. (CHARLIE BROWN *exits, but* SNOOPY *pauses, turns, and strikes a dramatic "thumbs down" pose to* LUCY) WELL, WHO ASKED YOU!

(SNOOPY *makes a hasty exit.* LUCY *stands center stage, figuring to herself on the clipboard and mumbling*) Now let's see. That's a fifty-one, "None of the above," and . . . (*She looks up*) Schroeder was right. I can already feel myself being filled with the glow of self-awareness. (PATTY *enters. She is heading for the other side of the stage, when* LUCY *stops her*) Oh, Patty, I'm conducting a survey and I wonder if . . .

PATTY

A hundred and ten, C, "Poor," "None of the above," "No," and what are you going to do about the dent you made in my bicycle!

(PATTY *storms off.* LUCY *watches her go then looks at the audience*)

LUCY

It's amazing how fast word of these surveys gets around.

(LINUS *wanders in and plunks himself down in front of the TV.* LUCY *crosses to him still figuring*)

LUCY

Oh, Linus, I'm glad you're here. I'm conducting a survey and there are a few questions I'd like to ask you.

LINUS

Sure, go ahead.

LUCY

The first question is: on a scale of zero to one hundred, with a standard of fifty as average, seventy-five as above average and ninety as exceptional, where would you rate me with regard to crabbiness?

LINUS

(Slowly turns his head to look at her, then turns back to the TV)

You're my big sister.

LUCY

That's not the question.

LINUS

No, but that's the answer.

LUCY

Come on, Linus, answer the question.

LINUS

(*Getting up and facing* LUCY)

Look, Lucy, I know very well that if I give any sort of honest answer to that question you're going to slug me.

LUCY

Linus. A survey that is not based on honest answers is like a house that is built on a foundation of sand. Would I be spending my time to conduct this survey if I didn't expect complete candor in all the responses? I promise not to slug you. Now what number would you give me as your crabbiness rating?

LINUS

(*After a few moments of interior struggle*)

Ninety-five.

(LUCY *sends a straight jab to his jaw which lays him out flat*)

LUCY

No decent person could be expected to keep her

word with a rating over ninety. (*She stalks off, busily figuring away on her clipboard*) Now, I add these two columns and that gives me my answer. (*She figures energetically, then finally sits up with satisfaction*) There, it's all done. Now, let's see what we've got. (*She begins to scan the page. A look of trouble skims over her face. She rechecks the figures. Her eternal look of self-confidence wavers, then crumbles*) It's true. I'm a crabby person. I'm a very crabby person and everybody knows it. I've been spreading crabbiness wherever I go. I'm a supercrab. It's a wonder anyone will still talk to me. It's a wonder I have any friends at all—(*She looks at the figures on the paper*) or even associates. I've done nothing but make life miserable for everyone. I've done nothing but breed unhappiness and resentment. Where did I go wrong? How could I be so selfish? How could . . .

(LINUS *has been listening. He comes and sits near her*)

LINUS

What's wrong, Lucy?

LUCY

Don't talk to me, Linus. I don't deserve to be spoken to. I don't deserve to breathe the air I breathe. I'm no good, Linus. I'm no good.

LINUS

That's not true, Lucy.

LUCY

Yes it is. I'm no good, and there's no reason at all why I should go on living on the face of this earth.

LINUS

Yes there is.

LUCY

Name one. Just tell me one single reason why I should still deserve to go on living on this planet.

LINUS

Well, for one thing, you have a little brother who loves you. (LUCY *looks at him. She is silent. Then she breaks into a great, sobbing "Wah!"*) Every now and then I say the right thing.

*(*LUCY *continues sobbing as she and* LINUS *exit. A brief musical interlude, a change of light, and* SCHROEDER *and* PATTY *come onstage)*

SCHROEDER

Of course it's surprising, but I'm sure Lucy knows now that she just can't be crabby any more. Where is everybody? I told them to be here. If we don't rehearse we can't sing at the assembly tomorrow. (*Calling off*) Charlie Brown, Linus, Lu . . .

LUCY

(*Offstage*)

Gimme that pencil, you blockhead!

LINUS

(Coming onstage)

No! Not until you give me back my crayons.

LUCY

(Coming onstage)

That's my best pencil, you block . . . (*She sees*

PATTY) If you don't give me that pencil, I'll tell Patty what you said about her!

SCHROEDER

Stop that. We've got to rehearse. You're late.

(He arranges them in a row with LINUS *between* PATTY *and* LUCY*)*

PATTY

What did you say about me, Linus?

LUCY

He said . . .

LINUS

Lucy!

SCHROEDER

Stop that!

CHARLIE BROWN

(*Running onstage*)

I'm sorry I'm late, but Snoopy and I were . . .

(SNOOPY *enters behind him)*

SCHROEDER

There's no time to be sorry.

PATTY

What did he say?

LUCY

He said . . .

SCHROEDER

Quiet! Now remember, this is a mood piece. We must paint a picture with music and words. And concentrate. (*He takes position as conductor and blows a note on his pitchpipe*) Remember, *adagio con brio.*

(They perform "The Glee Club Rehearsal." The subplot is carried on with a minimum of gesture and display, and those not directly involved in it are unaware that anything unusual is happening. SCHROEDER, *for instance, is oblivious of anything wrong until the very end. "Home, Home on the Range" is sung throughout; the other lines are sung simultaneously)*

ALL
(*Singing*)

Oh, give me a home
Where the buffalo roam,
Where the deer and the antelope play,

LUCY

Give me my pencil.

ALL

Where seldom is heard
A discouraging word,

LINUS

Not on your life.

ALL

And the skies are not cloudy all day.

(PATTY *and* LUCY *sing simultaneously*)

PATTY

If you don't tell me what you told Lucy
I'm just going to scream!

LUCY

Gimme my pencil, you blockhead!

ALL

Home,
Home on the range,

LUCY

(*Sings alone*)

Give me my pencil.

ALL

Where the deer and the antelope play.

LINUS

No!
Not until you promise not to tell her.

LUCY

What are you trying to do?
Stifle my freedom of speech?

ALL

Where seldom is heard

LUCY

Give me my pencil.

ALL

A discouraging word,

LINUS

No promise, no pencil.

ALL

And the skies are not
Cloudy all day.

PATTY

What pencil?

LINUS

(Looks at his hands and sees he is no longer holding the pencil)

No!

(PATTY victoriously holds up the pencil she has managed to sneak away from him. LINUS looks horrified at it)

ALL

Oh, give me a land,

LINUS

Give me that pencil!

(He grabs it back)

ALL

Where the bright diamond sand

PATTY

Linus, it just isn't fair!

SCHROEDER

Sing!

ALL
(With vigor)

Flows leisurely down the stream.

CHARLIE BROWN
(Leaning forward and whispering to LINUS*)*

Why did you take Patty's pencil?

LINUS
Aaugh!

(He stomps offstage in desperation)

ALL
Where the graceful white swan
Goes gliding along,

PATTY
(To LUCY*)*

What did he call me?

ALL

Like a maid in a heavenly dream.

LUCY

He said—
He said you were—an enigma.

PATTY

An enigma?

CHARLIE BROWN

An enigma?

SNOOPY

An enigma?

ALL

Home,
Home on the range,
Where the deer
And the antelope play.

PATTY

Boy, that makes me—

What a terrible thing to call a—
What's an enigma?
Never mind.

(*She stomps off after* LINUS)

LUCY

What's an enigma?

CHARLIE BROWN

What's an enigma?

SNOOPY

What's an enigma?

LUCY

Hey, he's still got my pencil!

(*She exits*)

ALL

Where seldom is heard
A discouraging word,

(CHARLIE BROWN *has become curious and slips out to follow the others)*

SCHROEDER

And the skies are not cloudy all day.

(SCHROEDER *discovers towards the middle of this line that he is the only one left singing except for the mournful, harmonic howls of the dog. As he watches in despair,* SNOOPY *finishes up the song, then tosses a congratulatory kiss to his conductor.* SCHROEDER *makes a hasty, explosive exit.* SNOOPY *retires to his doghouse*)

SNOOPY

Now why is it I always have my supper in the red dish and my drinking water in the yellow dish? One of these days I'm going to have my supper in the yellow dish and my drinking water in the red dish. Life is just too short not to live it up a little.

(SCHROEDER *and* LINUS *enter*)

SCHROEDER

Linus, did you fill out all those forms that Miss Othmar gave us in school today?

LINUS

Uh huh. I put down my name and address and our telephone number.

SCHROEDER

Well, what did you put where it says "family doctor"?

LINUS

I wasn't too sure, so I put down Dr. Seuss.

(LINUS *exits.* SCHROEDER *sits*)

SNOOPY

My teeth are tingling again. I feel like I've just got to bite somebody before sundown or I shall go stark raving mad. And yet I know that society frowns on such an action. So what happens? I'm stuck with tingly teeth.

(LUCY *enters and casually approaches* SCHROEDER)

LUCY

Psst. Hooray for Irving Berlin!

(LUCY *is off and running with* SCHROEDER *right behind her*)

SNOOPY

I hate cats. To me, cats are the crabgrass on the lawn of life. I am a cat-hater, a cat-despiser and a cat-loather. (*A burst of cats' yowling is heard offstage*) I'm also scared to death of them.

(LINUS *comes onstage with his blanket.* LUCY *and* PATTY *come onstage from another side and see him*)

LUCY

Oh, here comes my little baby brother, Linus, with his little blanket.

PATTY

There's your little baby brother with his silly little blanket.

LUCY

Well, you know how babies are with their baby blankets.

LINUS

(Flinging the blanket cape-style around his shoulders)

I am Count Dracula from Transylvania.

(LUCY *and* PATTY *immediately burst into screams and run offstage.* LINUS *happily skips off in another direction.* SNOOPY *is left*)

SNOOPY

Sometimes I think I'll just pull up stakes and move out of here. Broaden my horizons, meet new people. But something holds me here. Something binds me to this spot. (*He heaves a great sigh*) That old supperdish.

(The lights begin doing somersaults as the music swings into a bright and energetic rhythm. LUCY *comes onstage, pulling* LINUS *along by the hand. They meet* CHARLIE BROWN *and proceed into the song "Little-Known Facts")*

CHARLIE BROWN

Hi, Linus. Where are you going?

LINUS

Lucy's teaching me, Charlie Brown. She says a sister is responsible for the education of her little brother, so she's teaching me. Boy, is she intelligent.

LUCY

Come along, Linus.

(She sings)

Do you see this tree?
It is a fir tree.
It's called a fir tree
Because it gives us fur,
For coats.
It also gives us wool in the wintertime.

LINUS

I never knew that before. That's very interesting.

LUCY

This is an elm tree.
It's very little,
But it will grow up
Into a giant tree,

An oak.
You can tell how old it is by counting its leaves.

LINUS

Gosh, Lucy, that's fascinating.

CHARLIE BROWN
(Speaking)

Now, wait a minute, Lucy. I don't mean to interfere, but . . .

LUCY

And way up there,
Those fluffy little white things;
Those are clouds, they make the wind blow.
And way down there,
Those tiny little black things,
Those are bugs.
They make the grass grow.

LINUS

Is that so?

LUCY

That's right. They run around all day long, tugging and tugging at each tiny seedling until it grows into a great tall blade of grass.

LINUS

Boy, that's amazing.

CHARLIE BROWN

Oh good grief.

LUCY

(Singing)

And this thing here.
It's called a hydrant.
They grow all over
And no one seems to know just how
A little thing like that gives so much water.

Do you see that bird?
It's called an eagle.
But since it's little
It has another name, a sparrow.
On Christmas and Thanksgiving we eat them.

CHARLIE BROWN

Lucy, how can you say that! I'm sorry, but I just can't stand idly by and listen to you . . .

LUCY

And way up there,
The little stars and planets
Make the rain that falls in showers.
And when it's cold and winter is upon us,
The snow comes up,
Just like the flowers.

CHARLIE BROWN

Now, Lucy, I know that's wrong. Snow doesn't come up, it comes down.

LUCY

After it comes up the wind blows it around so it looks like it's coming down, but actually it comes up out of the ground like grass. It comes up, Charlie Brown, snow comes up!

CHARLIE BROWN

Oh good grief.

(He makes an agonized rush for the wings)

LINUS

Lucy, why is Charlie Brown banging his head against a tree?

LUCY

To loosen the bark so the tree will grow faster. Come along, Linus.

(They exit, the music flitting along behind them. Then a change. The atmosphere grays and a heavy, tired phrase repeats itself in the orchestra. SNOOPY *is prone on his house)*

SNOOPY

My stomach clock just went off. It's suppertime and Charlie Brown has forgotten to feed me. Here I lie, a withering hollow shell of a dog, and there sits my supperdish, empty. But that's all right. He'll remember. When no furry friend comes to greet him after school, *then* he'll remember. And he'll rush out here to the doghouse but it will be too late. There will be nothing left but the dried carcass of his former friend who used to run and play so happily with him. Nothing left but the bleached bones of . . .

*(*CHARLIE BROWN *has come onstage and is standing with* SNOOPY's *supperdish)*

CHARLIE BROWN

Hey, Snoopy. Are you asleep or something? I've been standing here for a whole minute with your supper and you haven't even noticed. It's supper-time.

(He sets the dish down. In an instant SNOOPY *is alert)*

SNOOPY

Suppertime? Suppertime!

(He strikes a magnificent pose on his roof-top and sings with a grand show of operatic fervor)

Behold the brimming bowl of meat and meal
Which is brought forth to ease our hunger.
Behold the flowing flagon moist and sweet
Which has been sent to slake our thirst.

CHARLIE BROWN

Okay, there's no need for a big production. Just get down off your doghouse and eat.

(CHARLIE BROWN *exits.* SNOOPY *slithers off his perch and proceeds into the song "Suppertime")*

SNOOPY
(Singing)

Suppertime.
Yes, it's suppertime,
Ooh, it's sup-sup-suppertime,
Very best time of day.
Suppertime.
Yeah, it's suppertime,
And when suppertime comes
Can supper be far away?

Bring on the soup dish,
Bring on the cup,
Bring on the bacon
And fill me up 'cause it's
Supper, supper, supper, suppertime.

(He fancyfoots with delight around the dish)

Br-r-ing on the dog food,
Bring on the bone,
Bring on the barrel and
Roll me home 'cause it's
Supper, supper, supper, supper.
Supper, super pepper-upper,
Supper, super-duper suppertime.

Wintertime's nice with the ice and snow,
Summertime's nice with a place to go,
Bedtime, overtime, halftime too,
But they just can't hold a candle to
My suppertime.
Oh yeah.

Br-r-ing on the hamburg,
Bring in the bun,
Pappy's little puppy loves everyone,
'Cause it's
Supper, supper, supper, supper,
Supper, super pepper-upper,
Supper, super-duper-dupper,
Dupa dupa dipa dapa, dipa dapa dupa dapa.

(SNOOPY *breaks into a wild, ecstatic dance,*

nearly bowling over CHARLIE BROWN *as he comes onstage*)

CHARLIE BROWN

Now wait a minute, Snoopy. Hey, you'll spill it all over. NOW CUT THAT OUT! (*Dog, music, action all stop in midphrase*) Why can't you eat your meal quietly and calmly like any normal dog.

(He exits)

SNOOPY

(Watches him go, then picks up his supperdish) So what's wrong with making mealtime a joyous occasion?

(He sings, quietly)

Doo doo doo, doo-de doo-doo doo.

(He disappears behind his house. The mood changes. The scene is dimmed and spotted with evening colors, and airy music is heard. LINUS *and* LUCY *wander on, looking at the sky)*

LUCY

Well, I don't know, Linus, it looks like an airplane to me the way the lights are blinking on and off. (SCHROEDER *and* PATTY *enter from the opposite side of the stage*) Schroeder, is that an airplane or a star?

SCHROEDER

I believe that is a star. But it could be a planet, you know. Or maybe even a satellite.

PATTY

It could be a satellite. I wonder.

LINUS

Well, we'll never find out by just sitting here.
(He crosses towards the front of the stage)

LUCY

Where are you going?

LINUS

I'm going over here to get a closer look.
(They all settle to enjoy the evening.

SNOOPY *climbs up on his doghouse, his empty supperdish in his mouth)*

SNOOPY

I like to sit up here after supper and listen to the sounds of the night. But somehow something seems to be missing. (*He lets forth a mournful howl*) In my opinion, that's exactly what was needed.

(CHARLIE BROWN *comes onstage, staring at a pencil in his hands, his face wide with wonder*)

CHARLIE BROWN

That little redheaded girl dropped her pencil. It has teeth marks all over it. She nibbles her pencil. She's human! Gosh, it hasn't been such a bad day after all.

(He and the others sing "Happiness")

CHARLIE BROWN

Happiness is finding a pencil.

SNOOPY

Sleeping in moonlight.

LINUS

Telling the time.

SCHROEDER

Happiness is learning to whistle.

LINUS

Tying your shoe
For the very first time.

PATTY

Happiness is playing the drum
In your own school band.

CHARLIE BROWN

And happiness is walking hand in hand.
Happiness is two kinds of ice cream.

LUCY

Knowing a secret.

SCHROEDER

Climbing a tree.

CHARLIE BROWN

Happiness is five different crayons.

SCHROEDER

Catching a firefly.

LINUS

Setting him free.

CHARLIE BROWN

Happiness is being alone every now and then.

ALL

And happiness is coming home again.

CHARLIE BROWN

Happiness is morning and evening,
Daytime and nighttime too.
For happiness is anyone and anything at all
That's loved by you.

LINUS

Happiness is having a sister.

LUCY

Sharing a sandwich.

LINUS *and* LUCY

Getting along.

ALL

Happiness is singing together
When day is through,
And happiness is those who sing with you.

Happiness is morning and evening,
Daytime and nighttime too.

CHARLIE BROWN

For happiness is anyone and anything at all
That's loved by you.

(Slowly the group gets up and leaves, nodding silent goodnights to each other. Finally, only CHARLIE BROWN *and* LUCY *are left—except for* SNOOPY, *asleep on his house.* LUCY *has been watching* CHARLIE BROWN. *At last she rises, walks resolutely towards*

him and extends her hand to him. Tentatively, almost fearfully, CHARLIE BROWN *takes it, and receives a firm, definitive handshake)*

LUCY

You're a good man, Charlie Brown.

(That's as much tenderness as LUCY *can allow herself. She quickly turns and makes her way offstage, leaving* CHARLIE BROWN *to mull it over, and perhaps even to arrive at a faint, glad smile as the curtains close)*

Snoopy—played here by Don Potter—a human being like any other dog. Or, if you like, the thinking dog's thinking dog. Through sheer force of imagination, Snoopy makes the world his own private stage. He can become a World War I pilot chasing the famous Red Baron without moving from the top of his doghouse. No other beagle can make that statement. He also has a cute smile.

Charlie Brown—played here by Alfred Mazza—the new hero of today. The disorganization man. Charlie Brown has never pitched a winning baseball game, has never been able to keep a kite in the air, has lost ten thousand checker games in a row, and has never successfully punted a football. Charlie Brown can do just about anything—the wrong way. That's what makes him so lovable.

Lucy—played here by Ann Gibbs *(center)*—is the dominating fussbudget who wants everything her way and often makes everything turn out that way. She is Charlie Brown's sounding board, reminding him of the human frailties that control us all. She is the resident headshrinker for the whole gang. Her fee is a nickel. She is just what the world needs, a good old-fashioned five-cent psychiatrist.

Linus—played here by Gene Kidwell—is the philosopher of the Peanuts gang. He likes to contemplate the marvels of the universe. Linus has an answer for everything and yet cannot rid himself of his security blanket. It is his way of coping with the real world.

Patty—played here by Karen Johnson—is Lucy's pal and co-plotter in the "war" against Charlie Brown. Patty is almost as constant as Lucy in undermining Charlie Brown's morale, but Lucy is still the champion ego buster. Patty thinks Snoopy is sweet however, and would kiss him if his face weren't so fuzzy. "The curse of a fuzzy face," Snoopy sighs.

Schroeder—played here by Jimmy Dodge—is the loner of the Peanuts group. He spends countless hours playing melodies by Beethoven on his toy piano, creating the music and the musings that flow from his imagination. Schroeder is the only one able to ignore Lucy's dominant personality because he has a mind of his own. Which is fortunate because Lucy would like to marry Schroeder.

Charlie Brown and Snoopy.